Vue.js Composition API

Cristian Salcescu

Vue.js Composition API

Vue.js Composition API

Cristian Salcescu

ISBN-13: 979-8680469828

History:

September 2020 First Edition

Contents

Preface

The Composition API provides a new way of managing reactivity. It is made of a set of Reactive API functions and plus the facility to register lifecycle hooks using imported functions.

In this book, we are taking a look at how to implement this Reactive API from scratch. Then we will implement a master-details functionality.

This book assumes you have knowledge of JavaScript. For a better understanding of the language consider reading Discover Functional JavaScript.

Source Code

The project files from this book are available at
https://github.com/cristi-salcescu/vue-composition-api.

Feedback

I will be glad to hear your feedback. For comments, questions, or suggestions regarding this book send me an email to cristisalcescu@gmail.com. Thanks in advance for considering to write a review of the book.

Fast Development Environment

The first thing we need to do is to set up our development environment.

Package Manager

A package manager is a tool used to track project dependencies in an easy to use manner. At the time of writing, Node.js package manager, in short npm, is the most popular. Let's start by installing Node.js.

The following commands can then be used in command prompt to check the Node.js and npm versions:

```
node --version
npm --v
```

NPM Packages

With `npm` we can install additional packages. These packages are the application dependencies. The installed packages can be found in the `node_modules` folder. The `--save` flag tells npm to store the package requirement in the `package.json` file.

The `package.json` file stores all the node packages used in the project. These packages are the application dependencies. The application can be shared with other developers without sharing all the node packages. Installing all the packages defined in the `package.json` file can be done using the `npm install` command.

Vue CLI

The easiest way to start with a Vue application is to use Vue CLI. First, ensure you have the latest Vue CLI installed

```
npm install -g @vue/cli
```

Then create a Vue project with the CLI using the following command:

```
vue create app
```

At the time of writing Vue 3 is not released yet, so use the CLI generate a Vue 3 Preview project.

Once the application is created the following commands can be used:

- `npm run serve`: compiles and hot-reloads for development
- `npm run build`: compiles and minifies for production

IDE

For code editing, we need an Integrated Development Environment, IDE in short.

I am going to use Visual Studio Code but feel free to use any editor you prefer.

To start the application, first, open the application folder in Visual Studio Code. Then start the terminal from Terminal -> New Terminal and run: `npm run serve`.

Chapter 01: Building a Reactive API

We start our learning journey by first understanding what reactivity is how is implemented in Vue 3. Imagine we have a simple `state` object and a `render` function.

```
const state = {
  message : "This is a message"
};

function render(state){
  document
  .getElementById("UI")
  .innerHTML =
    `<span>${state.message}</span>`;
}
```

Invoking the `render(state)` function displays the message in the UI.

```
render(state);
```

Now, suppose we modify the `message` property of the `state` object.

```
state.message = "A new message";
```

The change of the `state` object is not reflected in the UI. If we want that to happen we need to invoke again the `render` function.

```
state.message = "A new message";
render(state);
```

Proxy

We need a way to detect object changes and call the **render** function. The Proxy object can help achieve that.

The proxy object defines custom behavior for operations like getting or setting a property. The next example shows a proxy calling the **render** function on property changes.

```
const reactiveHandler = {
  set: function(obj, prop, value) {
    obj[prop] = value;
    render(obj);
    return true;
  }
};

const state = new Proxy({
  message: "This is a message"
}, reactiveHandler);
```

The **reactiveHandler** provides a handler for setting an object property. The handler changes the property, calls **render** with the modified object and returns **true** indicating a successful operation.

reactive()

Reactivity in Vue refers to the process of automatically updating the UI when the state object changes.

We can make an object reactive by simply using a new utility function wrapping the proxy call.

```
function reactive(obj){
  return new Proxy(obj, reactiveHandler);
}

const state = reactive({
  message: "This is a message"
});
```

The **reactive** function takes an object and returns a new proxy object wrapping it. All the interactions with the object, like setting and getting data, go through the proxy handler.

At this point, there is no need to manually call the `render` function when doing a change on the `state` object. The following change is reflected in the UI.

```
state.message = "A new message";
```

watchEffect()

This solution has a drawback. It explicitly states the function to be called. We want to be able to detect this subscriber function without explicitly invoking it in the proxy definition.

JavaScript is a single-threaded language. This means that a single function can execute at a specific moment. We can create a utility function that executes this function but also stores it in a variable.

Consider the following `watchEffect` utility function.

```
let currentFunc = null;

function watchEffect(f){
  currentFunc = f;
  f();
  currentFunc = null;
}
```

`watchEffect` takes a function `f`. It stores the function in the `currentFunc` variable, giving us access to the currently executing function. Then it executes the `f` function and resets the `currentFunc` variable to `null`.

Instead of executing the `render(state)` directly, we can call it using the `watchEffect` utility.

```
watchEffect(() => {
  render(state);
});
```

At this point, we have access to the currently executing function in the `reactiveHandler` handler.

The `get` handler returns the requested property and saves the currently executing function as the subscriber.

The `set` handler changes the property and calls the subscriber function registered in the `get` handler.

```
let subscriber = null;

const reactiveHandler = {
  get: function  (obj, prop) {
    if(currentFunc != null){
      subscriber = currentFunc;
    }
    return obj[prop];
  },
  set: function(obj, prop, value) {
    obj[prop] = value;
    subscriber(obj);
    return true;
  }
};
```

In this example, we don't need to specify the function to be called when the state changes. The function is automatically detected by wrapping its call inside the `watchEffect` utility.

Several Subscribers

The previous reactive handler supports only one subscriber function. We are going to fix this limitation and support multiple subscribers.

Instead of storing a single subscriber, we can use an array saving several subscribers. The `get` proxy handler adds subscribers to the list.

The `notify` function goes through all the subscribers and calls them with the provided object. The `set` handler calls `notify` with the changed object.

```
const subscribers = [];

function notify(obj){
  subscribers.forEach(fn => {
    fn(obj);
  });
}

const reactiveHandler = {
  get: function  (obj, prop) {
    if(currentFunc != null){
```

```
      subscribers.push(currentFunc);
    }
    return obj[prop];
  },
  set: function(obj, prop, value) {
    obj[prop] = value;
    notify(obj);
    return true;
  }
};
```

Several Objects

Our existing reactive utilities have another misbehavior. They register all subscribers to all reactive objects. Subscribers should be specific for each reactive object.

We can start by encapsulating the previous dependency management functionally in an object. The next Dependency class creates an object managing a list of subscribers. It allows us to add a new subscriber and to notify all subscribers.

```
class Dependency {
  constructor(){
    this.subscribers = [];
  }

  add(f){
    if(f != null){
      this.subscribers.push(f);
    }
  }

  notify(obj){
    this.subscribers.forEach(f => {
      f(obj);
    });
  }
}
```

We can improve the previous code by replacing the array with a Set. The difference is that a Set allows only unique values while the array doesn't have this constraint. The Set collection does not add callbacks that already exists in the collection.

```
this.subscribers = new Set();
```

The dependency object created with the `Dependency` class manages all dependencies for an object.

```
let dep = new Dependency();
```

To make sure we have different subscribers for each object we can use a WeekMap where the key is the object itself and the value is a dependency management object.

First, we create a WeekMap with the dependencies for all objects.

```
const depsMap = new WeakMap();
```

Then in the `get` handler, we take the current dependency management for that object. If it doesn't exist we create a new one. We use this dependency management object to add the new subscriber function.

```
const reactiveHandler = {
  get: function  (obj, prop) {
    let dep = depsMap.get(obj);
    if(!dep){
      dep = Dependency()
      depsMap.set(obj, dep)
    }
    dep.add(currentFunc);
    return obj[prop];
  },
  //...
};
```

In the `set` handler we get the dependency management for the current modified object and use it to notify all its subscribers.

```
const reactiveHandler = {
  //...
  set: function(obj, prop, value) {
    obj[prop] = value;
    const dep = depsMap.get(obj);
    dep.notify();
    return true;
```

```
  }
};
```

At this point, we have a system where each object has its own set of subscribers.

Deleting Properties

The `reactiveHandler` should also handle the case when a property is deleted. The proxy object allows us to define such a handler using the `deleteProperty` method.

The delete handler removes the requested property and notifies all the subscribers with the changed object.

```
const depsMap = new WeakMap();

const reactiveHandler = {
  //...
  deleteProperty(obj, prop) {
    if (obj.hasOwnProperty(prop)) {
      delete obj[prop];
      const dep = depsMap.get(obj);
      dep.notify();
    }
  }
};

const arr = reactive([1, 2, 3]);

watchEffect(() => {
  render(arr);
});

delete arr[0];
```

In JavaScript, arrays are emulated using objects. For this reason, the `reactive` utility using proxies works for both objects and arrays.

Reactive API

So far we have created a simplified version of the new Reactive API available in Vue 3.

The Reactive API has two main hook functions, `reactive` and `watchEffect` which are similar to the ones we have just implemented. Here is how we can use these hooks from Vue to create a reactive object and register a subscriber updating the UI.

```
import { reactive, watchEffect } from 'vue';

const state = reactive({
  message: "This is a message"
});

function render(state){
  document
  .getElementById("UI")
  .innerHTML =
    `<span>${state.message}</span>`;
}

watchEffect(() => {
  render(state);
});

state.message = "A new message";
```

`reactive` creates a reactive state object.

Rendering state in the UI is a side-effect. `watchEffect` allows us to run a side-effect that will then be executed again when the reactive state changes.

`watchEffect` gets a callback function and executes the function immediately. If the callback function uses a reactive object it registers the callback function as a dependency for that reactive object. When the reactive object changes the callback function is executed again.

Recap

Reactivity in Vue is about executing a dependent side-effect when an object changes. The core behavior is to update the UI when the associated state object is modified.

Proxy handlers allow us to register dependencies and to notify them when the object changes.

The `get` handler adds the currently executing function as the subscriber.

The `set` handler notifies all subscriber functions registered in the `get` handler.

The main reactive hooks in Vue are the `reactive` and `watchEffect` functions.

`reactive` returns a reactive object.

`watchEffect` executes and registers side-effect callbacks using reactive objects.

Chapter 02: Reactivity with Getters and Setters vs Proxies

The reactivity system in Vue 2 is implemented using getters and setters. We are going to create a simplified similar system and look at its limitations.

Getters/Setters

The utility function making objects reactive is called observable() in Vue 2. Here is how we can build it using an approach comparable to the one used to define the reactive function.

```
const depsMap = new WeakMap();

function observable(obj) {
  Object.keys(obj).forEach((prop) => {
    createReactiveProperty(obj, prop);
  });
  return obj;
}

function createReactiveProperty(obj, prop) {
  let value = obj[prop]
  Object.defineProperty(obj, prop, {
    get () {
      let dep = depsMap.get(obj);
      if(!dep){
        dep = new Dependency()
```

```
        depsMap.set(obj, dep)
      }
      dep.add(currentFunc);
      return value;
    },
    set (newValue) {
      value = newValue;
      const dep = depsMap.get(obj);
      dep.notify(obj);
    }
  });
}
```

The `observable` function takes an object and makes all of its properties reactive by creating a getter and a setter for each one.

The Object.defineProperty() method defines a new property on an object. It modifies the existing object, it doesn't create a new one.

Consider the following reactive object created with the `observable` function.

```
const fruit = observable({
  calories: 99,
  protein: 1.4
});
```

Here is how it looks after the new properties are added.

```
▼ {} 🔵
    calories: 99
    protein: 1.4
  ▶ get calories: ƒ ()
  ▶ set calories: ƒ (newValue)
  ▶ get protein: ƒ ()
  ▶ set protein: ƒ (newValue)
```

For each property, a new getter and a new setter are created.

The getter function registers the current function as a subscriber. The setter function calls all subscribers with the new modified object.

This approach has a few limitations. It cannot detect when a new property is added or when a property is deleted. This is why in Vue 2 we had to use

Vue.set to add a reactive property to an object and Vue.delete to remove an existing property.

Arrays

This technique implies that we need to create a getter and a setter for each property. This can become a problem for large arrays. This is a reason for which arrays are treated differently in Vue 2.

The observable utility does not create a getters-setter pair for each element in the array, but it just adds new behavior to all array methods.

In the next example, the observable utility creates a reactive object with the value property. The getter for the value property registers all the subscriber functions reading it. The value property stores the original array.

The reactive array is a wrapper around the original array. When we call the push method on the reactive array it invokes the same method on the original array but it also notifies all the existing subscribers.

```
const arrayPrototype = {
  value: null,
  push(newElement){
    this.value.push(newElement);
    const dep = depsMap.get(this);
    dep.notify(this);
  }
}

function observable(array) {
  const obj = Object.create(arrayPrototype);
  obj.value = array;
  createReactiveProperty(obj, 'value');
  return obj;
}
```

This approach works well when working with arrays using their methods but is unable to detect changes when assigning a value to a specific index, or when deleting an element at a specific index.

```
const arr = observable([1, 2, 3]);

watchEffect(() => {
```

```
  render(arr);
});

//Reactivity works
arr.push(4);

//Reactivity doesn't work
arr[0] = 100;
delete arr[0];

function render(arr){
  document
  .getElementById("UI")
  .innerHTML =
    `<span>${arr.value}</span>`;
}
```

Again for these situations in Vue 2, we use the Vue.set and Vue.delete helpers.

Proxies

All these problems are solved in Vue 3. Proxies are able to detect changes in arrays. Arrays are emulated in JavaScript using objects so the proxy handler can detect changes at a specific index.

The proxy handler can detect deletion. The same proxy getter and setter handlers are used for exiting or new properties.

The following code, updating and deleting elements from an array, requires the use of the special helpers in Vue 2.

```
<template>
  <div>
    <div
     v-for="number in numbers"
     :key="number" >
       {{ number }}
    </div>
    <button @click="generate">
      Generate
    </button>
    <button @click="deleteElement">
```

```
      Delete
    </button>
  </div>
</template>

<script>
import Vue from 'vue';

export default {
  data(){
    return {
      numbers: [0, 1]
    }
  },
  methods: {
    generate(){
      Vue.set(this.numbers, 0, Math.random());
    },
    deleteElement(){
      Vue.delete(this.numbers, 0);
    }
  }
}
</script>
```

The numbers property stores an array on the reactive state object.

The generate method changes the element at index 0 with a random number. The deleteElement removes the element at index 0.

The reactivity system using proxies does not handle these situations as special cases. The same functionality can be implemented in Vue 3 without using helpers.

```
export default {
  data(){
    return {
      numbers: [0, 1]
    }
  },
  methods: {
    generate(){
```

```
      this.numbers[0] = Math.random();
    },
    deleteElement(){
      delete this.numbers[1];
    }
  }
}
```

Recap

The reactivity system implemented with getters and setters cannot detect when new properties are added or deleted. Also, it is not practical to create a getter and a setter for each element in the array.

The reactivity system implemented with proxies doesn't have these limitations. Proxies can detect getting, setting, or deleting a property from both objects and arrays.

Chapter 03: Composition API

Next, we are going to look at how to create components using both the regular syntax and the new one using the Composition API.

Regular Syntax

Let's start by examining how to build a simple counter component using the regular syntax.

```
<template>
  <div>
    {{counter}}
    <button
     @click="increment">
       Increment
    </button>
    <button
     @click="decrement">
       Decrement
    </button>
  </div>
</template>

<script>
export default {
  data(){
    return {
      counter: 0
    }
```

```
  },
  methods: {
    increment(){
      this.counter += 1;
    },
    decrement(){
      this.counter -= 1;
    }
  }
}
</script>
```

This component has two options, `data`, and `methods`.

`data` is a function returning an object with all the reactive state. In our case, the state contains a single property `counter`. The `counter` is displayed in the template.

The `methods` option contains two methods updating the reactive state. They are used as handlers for the click events. Inside these methods, the `this` keyword gives access to the reactive data.

Composition API

The Composition API is made of a Reactive API plus a new set of lifecycle hooks.

Everything related to the Composition API happens inside the `setup` lifecycle hook. `setup` is the first hook called when an instance is created. Everything returned by `setup` is available in the template.

`setup` executes before all other lifecycle methods. It has no access to `this`.

reactive()

Here is how we can write the same counter component using the Composition API.

```
<template>
  <div>
    {{state.counter}}
    <button
     @click="increment">
```

```
        Increment
      </button>
      <button
       @click="decrement">
          Decrement
      </button>
    </div>
</template>

<script>
import { reactive } from 'vue';

export default {
  setup() {
    const state = reactive({
      counter: 0
    });

    function increment(){
      state.counter += 1;
    }

    function decrement(){
      state.counter -= 1;
    }

    return {
      state,
      increment,
      decrement
    }
  }
}
</script>
```

The reactive state containing the `counter` property is created using the `reactive` utility function inside the `setup` lifecycle hook. It is then returned and used in the template. The two functions changing the state are also defined in the `setup` hook and then returned and used in the template as event handlers.

The template is similar to the one implemented using the regular syntax. The only difference is that we have to use the whole state object to access the counter property.

```
<div>
  {{state.counter}}
</div>
```

This happens because we need to pass the whole state object from the setup hook.

```
setup() {
  const state = reactive({
    counter: 0
  });

  return {
    state
  }
}
```

We cannot use the spread syntax when returning the reactive state object. If we do that the object loses its reactivity.

```
return {
  ...state
}
```

The reactivity is also lost when we just extract a property from the state object and return it to be accessed in the template.

```
return {
  counter: state.counter
}
```

When we want to access a property from the reactive state object in the template without passing the whole state object we can use the toRefs utility.

toRefs converts each property of an object into a reactive reference.

```
import { reactive, toRefs } from 'vue';

setup() {
  const state = reactive({
```

```
    counter: 0
  });

  return {
    ...toRefs(state)
  }
}
```

ref()

ref creates a reactive reference. It wraps a primitive into a reactive object having the `value` property.

Next, you can check how to build the counter component using `ref` to create the reactive state.

```
<template>
  <div>
    {{counter}}
    <button
     @click="increment">
      Increment
    </button>
    <button
     @click="decrement">
      Decrement
    </button>
  </div>
</template>

<script>
import { ref } from 'vue';

export default {
  setup() {
    const counter = ref(0);

    function increment(){
      counter.value += 1;
    }

    function decrement(){
```

```
        counter.value -= 1;
    }

    return {
        counter,
        increment,
        decrement
    }
  }
}
</script>
```

ref takes a value and creates a reactive ref object wrapping that value. The ref object has a single property **value** that gives access to the inner value. The **value** property of the ref object is required only in the **setup** hook. The template automatically unwraps all the ref objects so there is no need to use the **value** property to access the inner value of a ref object.

In the template, we just use the ref object and we have access to its inner value.

```
<div>
  {{counter}}
</div>
```

Recap

The new Composition API syntax is additive in Vue 3. We can create components using the regular syntax or the new syntax.

The Composition API is used only inside the **setup** lifecycle hook.

reactive creates a reactive object.

ref creates a reactive reference.

The state and the functions modifying that state should be returned from the **setup** hook in order to be available in the template.

Destructuring or using the spread operator on a reactive object removes its reactivity. Don't do that. **toRefs** is useful when we want to destructure or use the spread syntax on the returned object without losing reactivity.

Chapter 04: Presentation Components

Starting from this point we are going to implement the book search functionality and we begin by creating the required presentation components.

Presentation components generate the UI using only their own props.

Presentation components just take in props and use them in the template. That makes them easier to reuse across the application. Presentation components don't have access to objects communicating to the external environment.

Item Component

Here a simple `BookItem` component displaying a book. It takes in the book in `props` and uses it to display the `title` and the `author` in the template.

Props can be declared as an array of strings.

```
<template>
  <div>
    <div>{{book.title}}</div>
    <div>{{book.author}}</div>
  </div>
</template>

<script>
export default {
  props: ['book']
}
```

```
</script>
```

We can list props also using an object. It defines a collection of key-value pairs. The key is the prop name, the value defines the prop type.

```
<script>
export default {
  props: {
    book: Object
  }
}
</script>
```

The style of the component is defined inside the `<style>` tag. In this case, we define the `.book-item` CSS class and then used it on the `<div>` element wrapping the book information.

```
<template>
  <div class="book-item">
    <div>{{book.title}}</div>
    <div>{{book.author}}</div>
  </div>
</template>

<script></script>

<style scoped>
.book-item {
  display: flex;
}

.book-item > div {
  flex: 1;
}
</style>
```

Root Component

Components are organized in a tree-like structure. This tree has a root component.

In our case, App is the root component. It creates a book object and sends it to BookItem component.

```
<template>
  <div id="app">
    <BookItem :book="book" />
  </div>
</template>

<script>
import BookItem from './components/BookItem.vue';

export default {
  components: {
    BookItem
  },
  setup() {
    const book = {
      title: 'The Cherry Orchard',
      author: 'Anton Chekhov'
    };

    return {
      book
    }
  }
}
</script>
```

Entry Point

In the application entry point, the `main.js` file the root component is created and rendered on the screen.

```
import { createApp } from 'vue';
import App from './App.vue'

createApp(App).mount('#app')
```

List Component

Next, let's add a list component.

The `BookList` component takes a list of books as props and shows it in the template.

```
<template>
  <div>
    <BookItem
     v-for="book in books"
     :key="book.id"
     :book="book" />
  </div>
</template>

<script>
import BookItem from './BookItem.vue';

export default {
  props: {
    books: Array
  },
  components: {
    BookItem
  }
}
</script>
```

The v-for directive renders the list of books using the BookItem component.

Root Component

Inside the setup hook, we create an array of books, return it, and then used it in the template.

```
<template>
  <div id="app">
    <BookList :books="books" />
  </div>
</template>

<script>
import BookList from './components/BookList.vue';

export default {
  components: {
    BookList
  },
```

```
  setup() {
    const books = [{
      title: 'The Cherry Orchard',
      author: 'Anton Chekhov'
    },
    {
      title: 'Ivanov',
      author: 'Anton Chekhov'
    }];

    return {
      books
    }
  }
}
</script>
```

Recap

Presentation components take in data props and use them in the template. They don't modify the external environment.

Presentation components are easier to reuse.

Chapter 05: Form Components

Next, we are going to look at how to create form components.

One thing that differentiates them from other components is that they have an internal state.

Form Template

The `BookSearch` is a form component. It allows the user to input the search criteria and creates the `query` object.

Form components wrap the input elements inside the `<form>` tag. In our case, we will use two inputs to search for books by title and author name.

```
<template>
  <form @submit.prevent="submit">
    <div>
      <label>Title:</label>
      <input
        type="search"
        v-model="state.title" />
    </div>
    <div>
      <label>Author:</label>
      <input
        type="search"
        v-model="state.author" />
    </div>
    <div>
      <button type="submit">
```

```
        Search
      </button>
    </div>
  </form>
</template>
```

The v-model directive establishes a two-way data binding between input values and state values.

Form State

Now we need to create the associated state.

reactive()

We can use the reactive utility to create a reactive state.

```
import { reactive } from 'vue';

export default {
  setup() {
    const state = reactive({
      title: '',
      author: ''
    });

    function submit(){
      const query = { ...state };
      console.log(query);
    }

    return {
      state,
      submit
    }
  }
}
```

We create a reactive state object with two properties using the reactive function. The submit function builds the query object by cloning all the existing state. The query object is just a plain data transfer object, we don't need reactivity on it. We should actually build it as a frozen object using Object.freeze.

To make the state and the `submit` function available in the template we return them from the `setup` hook.

ref()

We can also create a reactive state using the `ref` utility. This time we need two variables. Both variables have to be returned from the `setup` method. Note that when building the `query` object we use the `value` property of the ref objects to get their inner value.

```
<script>
import { ref } from 'vue';

export default {
  setup() {
    const title = ref('');
    const author = ref('');

    function submit(){
      const query = {
        title: title.value,
        author: author.value
      };
      console.log(query);
    }

    return {
      title,
      author,
      submit
    }
  }
}
</script>
```

In the template, we can access the state variables directly using their name. We don't need to use the `value` property.

```
<input
  v-model="title" />
```

```
<input
 v-model="author" />
```

Recap

Form components have associated state. We create a two-way data binding between the input values and the reactive state. This gives us access to the current value in the input by just using the associated state object.

We can use the `reactive` function and create one state object with a property for each input, or we can use the `ref` utility and build a state object for each input.

Chapter 06: Component Communication

The main idea in a component-based design is to split the page into small components easier to understand and reuse.

Splinting the page into smaller pieces creates the challenge of communicating between these parts.

This is what we are going to look next.

Props

Props are used to send data from parent to child components.

The `App` root component sends the list of books to the `BookList` component using props.

```
<BookList :books="books" />
```

Then the `BookList` component sends those books to the `BookItem` components.

```
<BookItem
  v-for="book in books"
  :key="book.id"
  :book="book" />
```

Here is how data flows from the root `App` component to the other child components.

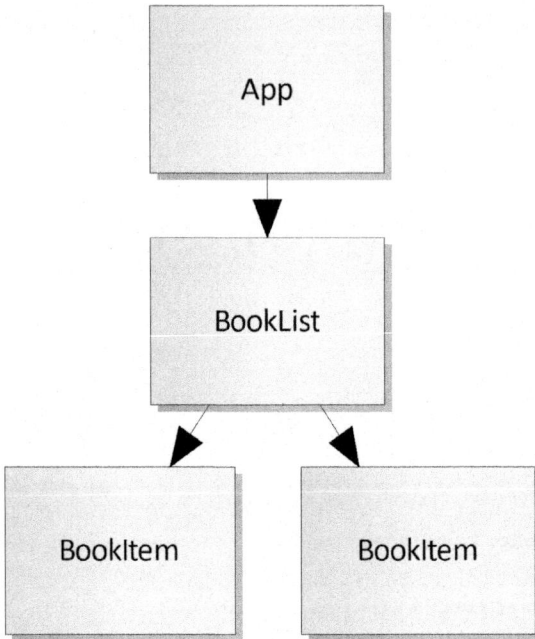

Events

Child components communicate with their parent using events.

The `setup` hook can get two parameters `props` and `context` as inputs. The `context` parameters allow us to emit events.

The `SearchBook` component emits the `search-by` event when the search button is clicked and this gives access to the current `query` object.

```
export default {
  setup(props, context) {
    const title = ref('');
    const author = ref('');

    function submit(){
      const query = {
        title: title.value,
        author: author.value
      };
      context.emit('search-by', query);
    }
```

```
    return {
      title,
      author,
      submit
    }
  }
}
</script>
```

context.emit('eventName', arg) emits an event. It can take a data object as a second argument for sending additional information related to the event.

In essence, we use props to get information in, and events to send data out.

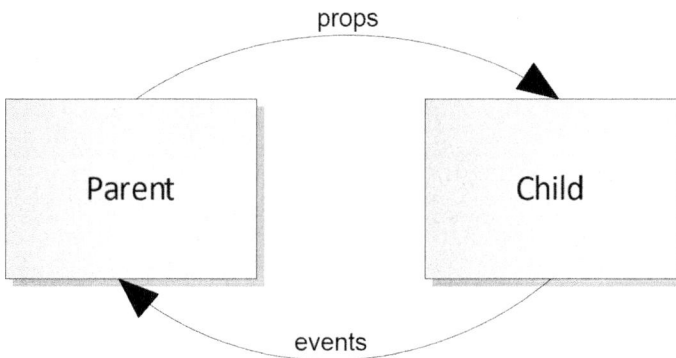

Root Component

In the App root component, we can handle the search-by event by setting a handler for it.

```
<BookSearch
 @search-by="filterBooks" />
```

In the root component, we create a list of books and return it from the setup hook.

We also define the filterBooks function and return it from setup to be used as an event handler in the template. At the moment it just logs the search query.

```
import BookSearch from './components/BookSearch.vue';
import BookList from './components/BookList.vue';

export default {
  components: {
    BookSearch,
    BookList
  },
  setup() {
    const books = [{
      id: 1,
      title: 'The Cherry Orchard',
      author: 'Anton Chekhov'
    },
    {
      id: 2,
      title: 'Ivanov',
      author: 'Anton Chekhov'
    }];

    function filterBooks(query){
      console.log(query);
    }

    return {
      books,
      filterBooks
    }
  }
}
```

Details Component

Next, we are going to introduce a new component BookDetails and see
how data can arrive at it. BookDetails is a presentation component that
takes in a detailed book object via props and displays more information
about the selected book.

```
<template>
  <div
    class="book-details"
```

```
  v-if="book">
   <div>{{book.title}}</div>
   <div>{{book.author}}</div>
   <div>
     <span>ISBN:</span>
     <span>{{book.isbn}}</span>
   </div>
   <div>
     <span>Pages:</span>
     <span>{{book.pages}}</span>
   </div>
   <div>
     <span>Publisher</span>
     <span>{{book.publisher}}</span>
   </div>
   <div>{{book.description}}</div>
  </div>
</template>

<script>
export default {
  props: ['book']
}
</script>
<style scoped>
.book-details {
  margin-top: 24px;
}
</style>
```

The v-if directive is used to do conditional rendering and display detailed information about the book only when one is provided.

Item Component

The list item component should allow us to select a book. For this, we add a new button to it that emits the **select** event using the **context** object.

```
<template>
  <div class="book-item">
    <div>{{book.title}}</div>
```

```
    <div>{{book.author}}</div>}
    <div><button @click="select">Select</button></div>
  </div>
</template>

export default {
  props: {
    book: Object
  },
  setup(props, context) {
    function select(){
      context.emit('select', props.book.id);
    }

    return {
      select
    }
  }
}
```

List Component

The list component handles the **select** event by re-triggering it. It does that by emitting a new event with an identical name and the same attached data.

```
<template>
  <div>
    <BookItem
      v-for="book in books"
      :key="book.id"
      :book="book"
      @select="select" />
  </div>
</template>

<script>
import BookItem from './BookItem.vue';

export default {
  props: {
```

```
      books: Array
    },
    components: {
      BookItem
    },
    setup(props, context) {
      function select(data){
        context.emit('select', data);
      }

      return {
        select
      }
    }
}
</script>
```

Root Component

In the root component, we handle the select event by logging the id of the book into the console.

```
<template>
  <div>
    <BookSearch
     @search-by="filterBooks" />
    <BookList
     :books="books"
     @select="selectBook" />
    <BookDetails />
  </div>
</template>

<script>
import BookSearch from './components/BookSearch.vue';
import BookList from './components/BookList.vue';
import BookDetails from './components/BookDetails.vue';

export default {
  components: {
    BookSearch,
```

```
    BookList,
    BookDetails
  },
  setup() {
    //...

    function selectBook(id){
      console.log(id)
    }

    return {
      books,
      filterBooks,
      selectBook
    }
  }
}
</script>
```

At this point, we know what book was selected and in the next chapters, we will look at how to get detailed information about this book and send it to the BookDetails component using props.

Here is how data travels from BookItem to BookList, then to App and arrives at the BookDetails component.

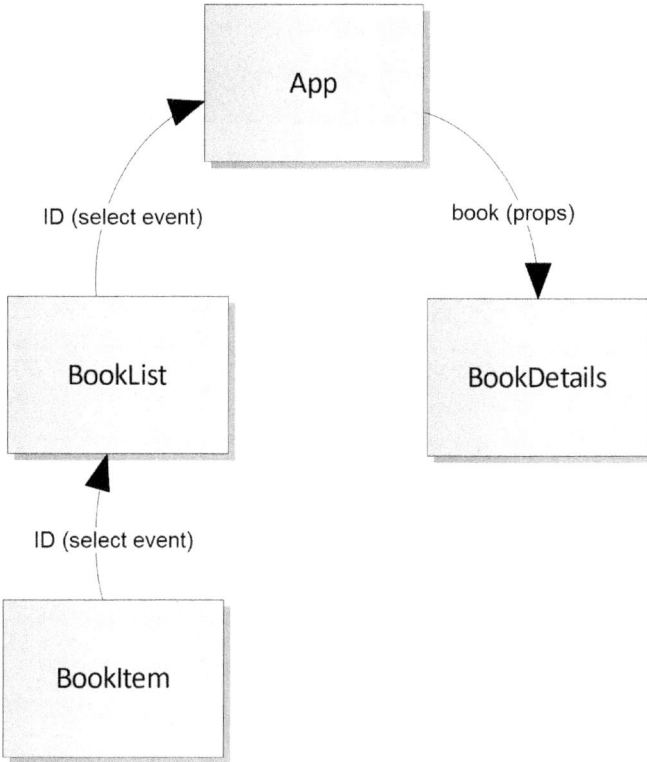

Recap

Parent components communicate with their child components using props. Props send data from parents to child components.

Child components interact with their parent using events. Events send data from child to parent components.

The **setup** hook can get the **props** and the **context** object as parameters. **context** allows us to emit events.

Chapter 07: Reactive Local State

Next, we are going to look at how to implement the book search and select functionalities. Both of them imply changing the UI based on user action.

Changing the UI means actually changing data.

Searching

Let's start with the search functionality. When the user presses the search button we need to display a new filtered list of books. To do that we need a new reactive state to store that filtered list.

We can define the `filteredBooks` property inside the `state` reactive object. Initially, it keeps all the books, but when the search button is clicked it is updated to reflect the search.

The `filterBooks` function updates the `filteredBooks` property. This function is then used as the event handler for the search click.

State is data that is stored and can change. In this example, the list with all books is not state. It is just a constant because it doesn't change. The filtered list of books is state because it changes based on the user search query.

```
import { reactive } from 'vue';

import BookSearch from './components/BookSearch.vue';
import BookList from './components/BookList.vue';
import BookDetails from './components/BookDetails.vue';

const books = [{
```

```
  title: 'The Cherry Orchard',
  author: 'Anton Chekhov'
},
{
  title: 'Ivanov',
  author: 'Anton Chekhov'
}];

function isInQuery(query){
  return function(book){
    return (
      (!query.title || book
        .title.toLowerCase()
        .includes(query.title.toLowerCase())) &&
      (!query.author || book
        .author.toLowerCase()
        .includes(query.author.toLowerCase())));
  };
}

export default {
  components: {
    BookSearch,
    BookList,
    BookDetails
  },
  setup() {
    const state = reactive({
      filteredBooks: books
    })

    function filterBooks(query){
      state.filteredBooks =
        books.filter(isInQuery(query));
    }

    return {
      state,
      filterBooks
    }
```

```
    }
}
```

isInQuery is a curried function that gets a query object and returns a function that takes a book and returns a boolean indicating if the book is included in the query.

isInQuery(query) returns a predicate function that is then used by the filter method on the books array.

In the template, we use state.filteredBooks to set the books property on the BookList component.

```
<template>
  <div id="app">
    <BookSearch
     @search-by="filterBooks" />
    <BookList
     :books="state.filteredBooks" />
  </div>
</template>
```

This solution works but it has a problem. We need to keep in sync any changes to the book collection or to the query object with the filtered list of books. Let's consider another approach that does that automatically for us.

computed()

We can take a distinct approach and just store the query object when the user clicks the search button. Then based on the list of books and the current query object we can compute the filtered list of books.

```
import { reactive, computed } from 'vue';

export default {
  setup() {
    const state = reactive({
      query: {},
      filteredBooks: computed(filterBooks)
    })

    function setQuery(query){
      state.query = query;
```

```
  }

  function filterBooks(){
    return books.filter(isInQuery(state.query));
  }

  return {
    state,
    setQuery
  }
 }
}
```

The `computed` function creates computed ref objects based on reactive state objects. When the dependent state changes the computed ref objects change also.

`computed` takes a getter function and returns an immutable reactive ref object. This object gives access to the returned value from the getter function.

Inside the `setup` hook the inner value of a computed property can be read using its `value` property.

`filteredBooks` is now a computed property. That means that when the `query` changes the `filteredBook` changes also. At the moment, the list of books is constant but in the next chapter, we will make it state. That means that when the list of books changes the filtered list also changes.

In a sense, computed properties can be used when we need state dependent on other state.

Below is the template using the `setQuery` function to handle the `search-by` event.

```
<template>
  <div id="app">
    <BookSearch
     @search-by="setQuery" />
    <BookList
     :books="state.filteredBooks" />
  </div>
</template>
```

Selecting an Item

Selecting an item is also about changing the state to hold the new book. We need a new property `selectedBook` on the reactive `state` object. The `selectBook` function at the moment updates the book with the new `id`. In the next chapter we will make a network call and set the detailed book.

```
export default {
  setup() {
    const state = reactive({
      query: {},
      filteredBooks: computed(filterBooks),
      selectedId: 0
    })

    function setQuery(query){}
    function filterBooks(){}

    function selectBook(id){
      state.selectedBook = {id}
    }

    return {
      state,
      setQuery,
      selectBook
    }
  }
}
```

In the template, we use `selectBook` function as a handler for the `select` event. Then we send the `state.selectedBook` value to the details component using props.

```
<template>
  <div>
    <BookList
      :books="state.filteredBooks"
      @select="selectBook" />
    <BookDetails
      :book="state.selectedBook" />
  </div>
```

```
</template>
```

Recap

State is data that is stored and can change.

The `reactive` utility can define reactive local state inside components. The `computed` utility defines computed properties that adjust automatically when the dependent state is modified.

Changing the UI means changing the state.

Chapter 08: Fetching Data

Till now we have hardcoded the list books inside the root component. In practice, we take these books from a web API.

Next, we are going to look at how to fetch and store that data inside the root component.

API Util

First, we need a function that makes the fetch request and retrieves the books from a web API. A simple fake REST API can be created using JSON server.

The `fetchBooks` function makes a network request using the fetch API and retrieves the list of books.

```
const baseUrl = "http://localhost:3000";

function toJson(response){
  return response.json();
}

function fetchBooks(){
  return fetch(`${baseUrl}/books/`)
    .then(toJson)
}

export default { fetchBooks };
```

Fetching List

Inside the root component, we use the result from the API call to update the `books` property on the reactive `state` object.

```
import api from './api/booksAPI';

//...

api.fetchBooks().then(data => {
  state.books = data;
});
```

Notice that till now the list of books didn't change. It was just a constant inside our application. Once the list of books can change it becomes state.

Here is the logic inside the root component storing all the books and the query object as state and computing the `filteredBooks` based on both of them.

```
import { reactive, computed } from 'vue';
import api from './api/booksAPI';

function isInQuery(query){}

export default {
  components: {
    BookSearch,
    BookList,
    BookDetails
  },
  setup() {
    const state = reactive({
      books: [],
      query: {},
      selectedBook: null,
      filteredBooks: computed(filterBooks)
    });

    function setQuery(query){}
    function selectBook(id){}

    function filterBooks(){
      return state.books.filter(isInQuery(state.query));
    }

    api.fetchBooks().then(data => {
```

```
      state.books = data;
    });

    return {
      state,
      setQuery,
      selectBook
    }
  }
}
```

Lifecycle Hooks

Inside the `setup` function, we can use lifecycle hooks like `onMounted`, `onUpdated`, `onUnmounted`. To do that we simply import the `onLifecycleEvent` functions and use them inside `setup`.

Below is an example of making an API call after the component was mounted.

```
import { reactive, computed, onMounted } from 'vue';

export default {
  setup() {
    //...

    onMounted(() => {
      api.fetchBooks().then(data => {
        state.books = data;
      });
    });

    return {
      state,
      setQuery,
      selectBook
    }
  }
}
```

Fetching Details

Next, we are going to retrieve the book details.

API Util

We need a new API utility function that fetches the complete book.

```
const baseUrl = "http://localhost:3000";

function toJson(response){}
function fetchBooks(){}

function fetchBook(id){
  return fetch(`${baseUrl}/books/${id}`)
    .then(toJson)
}

export default { fetchBooks, fetchBook };
```

Root Component

In the root component, we have to change the `selectBook` function used as the event handler for the `select` event.

`selectBook` gets the `id` of the book, makes the network call to retrieve the book details, and updates the `selectedBook` property on the reactive `state` object.

```
<template>
  <div id="app">
    <BookSearch
     @search-by="setQuery" />
    <BookList
     :books="state.filteredBooks"
     @select="selectBook" />
    <BookDetails
     :book="state.selectedBook" />
  </div>
</template>

<script>
import BookSearch from './components/BookSearch.vue';
```

```
import BookList from './components/BookList.vue';
import BookDetails from './components/BookDetails.vue';

import { reactive, computed } from 'vue';
import api from '@/api/booksAPI';

function isInQuery(query){}

export default {
  components: {
    BookSearch,
    BookList,
    BookDetails
  },
  setup() {
    const state = reactive({
      books: [],
      query: {},
      selectedBook: null,
      filteredBooks: computed(filterBooks)
    });

    function setQuery(query){}
    function filterBooks(){}

    onMounted(() => {});

    function selectBook(id){
      if(id){
        api.fetchBook(id)
          .then(newBook => state.selectedBook = newBook);
      }
    }

    return {
      state,
      setQuery,
      selectBook
    }
  }
```

```
}
</script>
```

watchEffect()

Next, we are going to look at another approach for taking the book details. This time the `BookDetails` component takes in the book `id`, fetches the details, and then renders the book.

It turns out that `props` are also reactive in the sense we can watch for changes. We can use `watchEffect` to run a specific piece of code whenever the book `id` changes. Here is how we can fetch the book details when the `id` changes inside the `BookDetails` component.

```
import { ref, watchEffect } from 'vue';
import api from '../api/booksAPI';

export default {
  props: ['id'],
  setup(props) {
    const book = ref(null);

    watchEffect(()=>{
      if(props.id){
        api.fetchBook(props.id)
          .then(data => { book.value = data; });
      } else {
        book.value = null;
      }
    });

    return {
      book
    }
  }
}
```

watch()

A similar solution can be implemented using the `watch` API. This is the direct equivalent of the `watch` option.

watch requires to specify the reactive property to watch for. It does not detect the reactive dependencies like watchEffect does. It takes two arguments.

The first argument is the data source watcher. This can be a reactive object or a function returning the watched value.

The second argument is the side-effect callback to run when the property changes. The callback is invoked only when the watched source has modified. It gets as inputs both the current and the previous value of the watched state.

The id itself is not a reactive object, the props object is. To watch for id changes we create a function returning the id from props.

```
watch(
  () => props.id,
  (id, prevId) => {
    console.log(id, prevId)
  }
);
```

The alternative is to watch the whole props object which is reactive. It can be passed to the watch function as the first argument. Then we can get the id from props when needed.

```
watch(
  props,
  props => {
    console.log(props.id)
  }
);
```

Here is how we can re-write the logic inside the BookDetails component using the watch API.

```
import { ref, watch } from 'vue';
import api from '../api/booksAPI';

export default {
  props: ['id'],
  setup(props) {
    const book = ref(null);
```

```
watch(
  () => props.id,
  id => {
    if(id){
      api.fetchBook(id)
        .then(data => { book.value = data; });
    } else {
      book.value = null;
    }
  }
);

return {
  book
}
}
}
```

Note that `watchEffect` runs the side-effect callback when invoked. This is how it detects the reactive dependencies. `watch` doesn't do that. It already knows what is the reactive object to look for.

Recap

We can fetch data inside the `setup` hook and update the reactive state.

Props are reactive so we can watch for changes using `watch` and `watchEffect`.

When data doesn't change is just a constant. Once it changes it becomes state.

Chapter 09: Reactive External State

The Composition API allows us to extract the logic from the **setup** hook into separate files and reuse it where is needed.

Extract Logic Out

Let's do just that and extra all the code from the **setup** hook in a new function called **useBooks**. Here is how it looks like.

```
import { reactive, computed } from 'vue';
import api from '@/api/booksAPI';

function isInQuery(query){}

function useBooks() {
  const state = reactive({
    books: [],
    query: {},
    filteredBooks: computed(filterBooks),
    selectedBook: null
  });

  function setQuery(query){}
  function selectBook(id){}
  function filterBooks(){}

  api.fetchBooks().then(data => {
    state.books = data;
  });
```

```
  return {
    state,
    setQuery,
    selectBook
  }
}
```

```
export default useBooks;
```

Now in the root component, we can simply use this function to enable the previous functionalities.

```
import useBooks from './business/useBooks';
```

```
export default {
  setup() {
    const { state, setQuery, selectBook } = useBooks();

    return {
      state,
      setQuery,
      selectBook
    }
  }
}
```

When using all the properties returned by the useBooks function we can simply apply the spread operator inside the returned object from the setup hook.

```
import useBooks from './business/useBooks';
```

```
export default {
  setup() {
    return {
      ...useBooks()
    }
  }
}
```

No changes are needed to the template. After refactoring, the setup function returns the same state object and functions.

Store

The previous `useBooks` creates a new state object and a new set of
functions wrapping it every time is called. In our case, we just need to
create this object managing the state once and use it in any component.

The next `BookStore` function creates an object managing state. This
store object does no longer make the network call at creation but offers a
new method `fetchBooks` that can be used inside components to do that.

```
import { reactive, computed } from 'vue';
import api from '@/api/booksAPI';

function isInQuery(query){}

function BookStore() {
  const state = reactive({
    books: [],
    query: {},
    selectedBook: null,
    filteredBooks: computed(filterBooks)
  });

  function setQuery(query){}
  function selectBook(id){}
  function filterBooks(){}

  function fetchBooks(){
    api.fetchBooks().then(data => {
      state.books = data;
    });
  }

  return {
    state,
    setQuery,
    selectBook,
    fetchBooks
  }
}
```

We invoke the `BookStore` function to create the store and then export it

from the store file. This way we are going to have only one store object
build by the `BookStore` function inside the application.

```
const bookStore = BookStore();
export default bookStore;
```

Inside the root component, we import the store object and destructure
out the required state and methods.

```
import bookStore from './business/bookStore';

export default {
  setup() {
    const { state, setQuery, selectBook, fetchBooks }
      = bookStore;

    fetchBooks();

    return {
      state,
      setQuery,
      selectBook
    }
  }
}
```

provide() / inject()

Next, we are going to look at another option for creating and making the
store available to all components.

The `provide` and `inject` utility functions allow us to pass values from
the parent component to any nested child components.

`provide` takes a key and a value. The key can be of any type.

`inject` takes a key and returns the associated value. If the key is not
found it returns `undefined`. It accepts an optional second argument as
the default value. In this case, when the key is not found it returns the
default value.

`provide` and `inject` can be invoked only inside the `setup` hook.

Knowing all this, we can create the store in the root component. This
may be handy when it requires additional arguments at creation.

```
const bookStore = BookStore();
provide("bookStore", bookStore);
```

Then we can access the store in any component by invoking the `inject` function with the right key.

```
const bookStore = inject("bookStore");
console.log(bookStore)
```

Parent components are the dependency providers for all their children, regardless of the child component hierarchy. The parent component uses the `provide` function to provide the data and the child component uses the `inject` function to access that data.

Recap

The Composition API allows us to write Vue related logic outside of components. It enables us to create reusable, self-contained pieces of business logic that can be hidden behind a friendly API.

The state and functions managing that state can be extracted out of components in functions like `useBooks`. These types of functions create a new local state every time they are invoked.

With the Composition API, we can split the state management logic between different store objects and then share this logic within components.

The `provide` and `inject` utility functions enable a dependency injection system.

Chapter 10: Central Store

Next, we are going to look at how to build a central store similar to Vuex using the Composition API.

State

This time we have a single state object storing all the application data that can change. It can be created using the **reactive** helper function.

```
import { reactive } from 'vue';

const state = reactive({
  books: [],
  query: {},
  selectedBook: null
});

export default state;
```

Getters

Getters are needed when we want to compute a derivated state. In our case, we need to compute the filtered list of books based on the current list of books and the current query.

Getters can be created as computed properties.

```
import { computed, toRefs } from 'vue';
import state from './state';

const getters = {
  books: computed(() => filterBooks(state))
};
```

```
function filterBooks({books, query}){
  return books.filter(isInQuery(query));
}

function isInQuery(query){}

export default getters;
```

There are cases when we just need to read a value from the store without computing any derived state. We shouldn't give access to the `state` object because it can be misused and modified.

toRef()

One option is to use the `toRef` utility.

`toRef` creates a ref to a property on a reactive source object. Check the new `selectedBook` property.

```
import { computed, toRef } from 'vue';
import state from './state';

const getters = {
  books: computed(() => filterBooks(state)),
  selectedBook: toRef(state, 'selectedBook')
};
```

It looks nice but the problem of modifying the `selectedBook` is still there.

The ref maintains the connection to its source property. When the source is modified the ref is also modified. When the ref is modified the source property is modified.

```
import {reactive, toRef} from 'vue';

const state = reactive({
  selectedBook : {id: 1}
})

const getters = {
  selectedBook: toRef(state, 'selectedBook')
};
```

```
state.selectedBook = {id: 2};
console.log(getters.selectedBook.value)
// { id: 2 }

getters.selectedBook.value = {id: 3};
console.log(state.selectedBook)
// { id: 3 }
```

computed()

It is possible to utilize another computed property returning the required value from the state object.

```
import { computed } from 'vue';
import state from './state';

const getters = {
  books: computed(() => filterBooks(state)),
  selectedBook: computed(() => state.selectedBook)
};
```

readonly()

A different choice is to give access to a read-only object reflecting the source state.

readonly takes an object and returns a read-only proxy to the original. Any nested property is read-only as well.

```
import { computed, readonly} from 'vue';
import state from './state';

const getters = {
  state: readonly(state),
  books: computed(() => filterBooks(state))
}
```

Note in the next example that trying to change the read-only proxy results in a warning.

```
import {reactive, readonly} from 'vue';

const state = reactive({
```

```
  selectedBook : {id: 1}
})

const getters = {
  state: readonly(state)
};

state.selectedBook = {id: 2};
console.log(getters.state.selectedBook)
// { id: 2 }

getters.state.selectedBook = {id: 3};
//Set operation on key "selectedBook" failed: target is readonly.
console.log(state.selectedBook)
// { id: 3 }
```

Mutations

Mutations are functions that enable us to change the state. This is the only place where the state can be modified.

```
import state from './state';

function setBooks(books){
  state.books = books;
}

function setQuery(query){
  state.query = query;
}

function setSelectedBook(newBook){
  state.selectedBook = newBook;
}

export default {
  setBooks,
  setQuery,
  setSelectedBook
}
```

Actions

Actions allow us to do asynchronous operations like fetching data and then execute mutations.

```
import api from '../api/booksAPI';
import mutations from './mutations';

function fetchBooks(){
  return api
    .fetchBooks()
    .then(mutations.setBooks);
}

function selectBook(id){
  if(id){
    api.fetchBook(id)
      .then(mutations.setSelectedBook);
  }
}

export default {
  fetchBooks,
  selectBook
};
```

fetchBooks makes a network request then saves the result in the store using the setBooks mutation.

selectBook fetches the book details then saves the returned data using the setSelectedBook mutation.

Root Component

Inside the root component, we can read data from the store using getters and use mutations and actions as event handlers.

```
<template>
  <div id="app">
    <BookSearch
     @search-by="mutations.setQuery" />
    <BookList
     :books="getters.books"
```

```
   @select="actions.selectBook" />
  <BookDetails
   :book="getters.selectedBook" />
 </div>
</template>
```

The root component imports getters, mutations, and actions from the store and returns them from the setup hook making them available in the template.

```
import actions from './store/actions';
import mutations from './store/mutations';
import getters from './store/getters';

export default {
  setup() {
    actions.fetchBooks();

    return {
      getters,
      mutations,
      actions
    }
  }
}
```

Connected Components

Next, let's look at a different approach where components are directly connected to the store.

Item Component

This time, the item component doesn't emit an event but invokes the selectBook action.

```
import actions from '@/store/actions';

export default {
  props: ['book'],
  setup() {
    return {
```

```
      select: actions.selectBook
    }
  }
}
```

List Components

The list component reads the list of books directly from the store using getters.

```
import getters from '@/store/getters';

export default {
  setup() {
    return {
      books: getters.books
    }
  }
}
```

Details Component

The details component reads the selected book from the store using getters.

```
import getters from '@/store/getters';

export default {
  setup() {
    return {
      book: getters.selectedBook
    }
  }
}
```

Form Search Component

The search component doesn't emit an event but invokes the setQuery mutation with the new query object.

```
import { ref } from 'vue';
import mutations from '@/store/mutations';

export default {
```

```
setup() {
  const title = ref('');
  const author = ref('');

  function submit(){
    const query = {
      title: title.value,
      author: author.value
    };
    mutations.setQuery(query);
  }

  return {
    title,
    author,
    submit
  }
}
}
```

Root Component

When components are connected to the store, the root component doesn't need to send them the necessary data or to handle the events and make the required changes to the store.

```
<template>
  <div>
    <BookSearch />
    <BookList />
    <BookDetails />
  </div>
</template>
```

The root component calls the fetchBooks action in the setup hook.

```
import BookSearch from './components/BookSearch.vue';
import BookList from './components/BookList.vue';
import BookDetails from './components/BookDetails.vue';

import actions from './store/actions';
```

```
export default {
  name: 'app',
  components: {
    BookSearch,
    BookList,
    BookDetails
  },
  setup() {
    actions.fetchBooks();
  }
}
```

Recap

With the Composition API, we can replicate the Vuex functionality and create a central store that contains four pieces: state, getters, mutations, and actions.

The state can be created using the `reactive` utility.

Getters defining a derived state can be created using the `computed` function.

Mutations are functions controlling how the state changes.

Actions are functions that can do asynchronous operations and then invoke mutations.

What's next?

For a more in-depth look at JavaScript and main functional principles, you may read Discover Functional JavaScript. Here, you will find more on pure functions, immutability, currying, decorators but also ideas on how to make code easier to read.

In the Functional Programming in JavaScript book you will find how to use JavaScript as a functional programming language by disabling the 'this' keyword and enforcing immutable objects with a linter. You will learn how to use statements like `if` and `switch` in a functional way, or how to create and use functors and monads.

If you want to learn how to build modern React applications using functional components and functional programming principles, you can consider reading Functional React, 2nd Edition.

Enjoy the learning journey!

About the author

Cristian Salcescu is the author of Discover Functional JavaScript.
He is a Technical Lead passionate about front-end development and enthusiastic about sharing ideas. He took different roles and participated in all parts of software creation. Cristian Salcescu is a JavaScript trainer and a writer on Medium.

Printed in Great Britain
by Amazon

82035167R00058